First published in 2006 by

Franklin Watts

338 Euston Road

London NW1 3BH

Franklin Watts Australia

Hachette Children's Books

Level 17/207 Kent Street

Sydney NSW 2000

Editor: Jennifer Schofield

Consultant: Steve Watts

(FRGS, Principal Lecturer University of Sunderland)

Art director: Jonathan Hair

Design: Mo Choy

Artwork: Ian Thompson

Picture researcher: Kathy Lockley

Acknowledgements:

Altitude/Still Pictures 15. Jacques Descloitres, MOBIS Land Rapid Response Team/NASA/GSFC 27. Michael & Patricia Fogden/Minden/Frank Lane Picture Agency 29. Michael Graber/Still Pictures 13. David T. Grewcock/Frank Lane Picture Agency 19. Robert Harding Picture Library 21, 22, 37, 38. Ian Harwood/Ecoscene 24. Dennis Johnson/Lonely Planet Images 16. c.Andrew K/epa/epa/Corbis 33. Chris Knapton/Science Photo Library 6. Wayne Lawler/Ecoscene 41. Alberto Nardi/NHPA 11. Mark Newman/Frank Lane Picture Agency 3b, 35, Cover. Fritz Polking/Ecoscene 25. c.Reuters/Corbis 32. Kevin Schafer/NHPA 8. Erik Schaffer/Ecoscene 43. c. Dennis Scott/Corbis 3t, 4/5, 44/5, 46/7, Cover. Bob Watkins/Photofusion 40. Martin Wendler/NHPA 30. David Woodfall/Still Pictures 42.

Every attempt has been made to clear copyright.

Should there be any inadvertent omission please

apply to the publisher for rectification.

A CIP catalogue record for this book

is available from the British Library.

ISBN 10: 0 7496 6784 2

ISBN 13: 978 0 7496 6784 9

Dewey Classification: 551.41

Printed in China

Franklin Watts is a division of Hachette Children's Books.

Understanding
LANDFORMS

Barbara Taylor

W
FRANKLIN WATTS
LONDON•SYDNEY

Contents

What shapes the land?

Landforms are natural features, such as cliffs or volcanoes, on the Earth's surface. They are caused by powerful forces deep inside the Earth, and by wind and water carving the land surface into new shapes. Understanding the shape of the land helps people to survive floods, earthquakes and other natural disasters. It also helps people to plan building projects, protect water supplies and decide on sustainable ways of using the land that will protect it for the future.

Understanding landforms helps people to build roads and other structures in the right place. They, in turn, change the shape of the land.

crust

mantle

outer core

inner core

CHANGING SHAPE

The shape of the land is changing all the time. Heat rising from the hot centre, or core, of the Earth pushes the surface up into mountains and causes volcanoes to erupt. It also moves land on the surface of the Earth sideways and tears it apart. On the surface, wind and water wear away the land in some places and build it up in others.

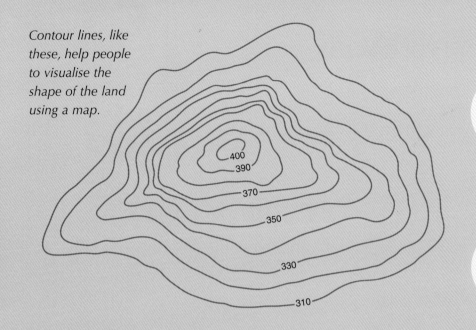

Contour lines, like these, help people to visualise the shape of the land using a map.

400
390
370
350
330
310

HELPING HAND
Throughout this book, this helping hand will give you useful tips and hints.

WARNING SIGN
When you see this sign, you should be extra careful when completing the task.

HOW HIGH IS THE LAND?

You can find out more about the ups and downs of the land by drawing a line graph using a map. On a map, thin brown lines join up places that are the same height above sea level. These brown lines are called contour lines. If the contour lines are close together, the land is steep and hilly.

Using the sample of contours above, trace the contour lines onto a piece of tracing paper. Turn the tracing over, place it on top of a blank piece of paper and rub firmly over the lines with a soft pencil to transfer them to the paper. Mark the height above sea level on each contour.

Now, draw a graph like the example below, but use your measurements.

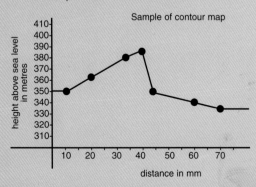

Sample of contour map

height above sea level in metres

410
400
390
380
370
360
350
340
330
320
310

10 20 30 40 50 60 70

distance in mm

Use a ruler to draw a straight line across the middle of your contour lines. On the line graph, plot the point where each contour line crosses the straight line. When you join up the points, you should be able to see the shape of the land as if you were standing in the countryside looking at it side on. Use the scale on the map to work out how large the hill is in metres. Look at some contour maps of your local area. Try to visualise the shape of the land by studying the pattern of the contour lines.

KEY SKILLS

Throughout this book, you will learn different skills. Each different skill is represented by one of the following icons:

 Completing a practical activity

 Working with graphs, maps, diagrams and photographs

 Researching information

 Analysing information

 Looking at global issues

Observing

7

Earth's jigsaw

The surface, or crust, of the Earth is broken up into huge plates, which fit together like the pieces of a jigsaw. Most of the plates include some large areas of land (continents) and some areas of ocean.

CONTINENTAL DRIFT

The crustal plates move a few centimetres every year because of hot, semi-liquid rocks (magma) in a layer under the Earth's crust called the mantle. The hot magma and gases churn around making the continents shift slowly. This process is called continental drift. It is believed that about 200 million years ago all the continents were joined together, but now some have drifted apart.

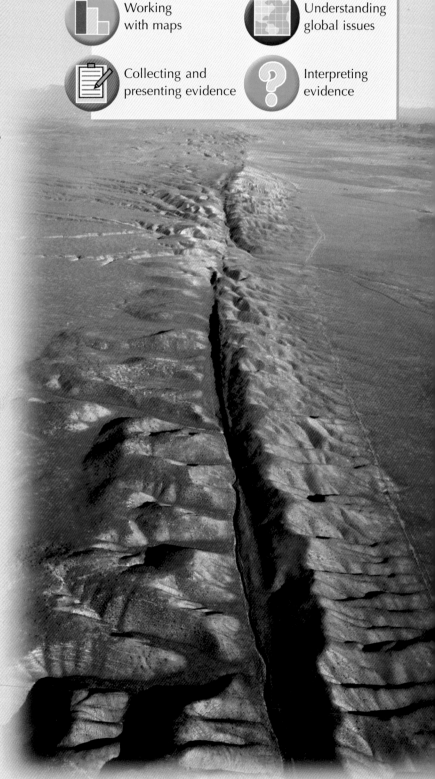

The San Andreas fault, USA. On the west coast of North America, the North American and Pacific plates are sliding slowly past each other. Movement along this fault line has caused major earthquakes.

WHAT HAPPENS WHERE PLATES MEET?

Three main things happen when plates meet at plate boundaries, or margins. The plates may move apart, move together or slide past each other.

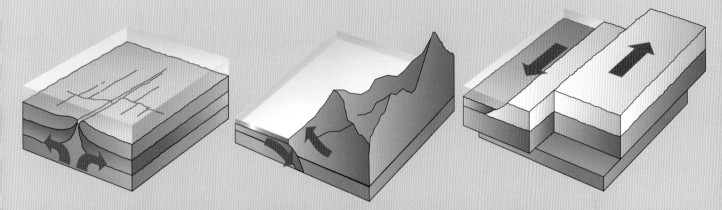

CONSTRUCTIVE BOUNDARY

Most crustal plates move apart under the oceans. Magma wells up into the gap, then cools and hardens to form lines of undersea mountains. This is called a constructive boundary, because new crust is formed, or constructed.

DESTRUCTIVE AND COLLISION BOUNDARIES

When crustal plates move together, the crust may melt and be destroyed, forming a destructive boundary. Sometimes the crust can crumple up to make mountains, forming a collision boundary.

CONSERVATIVE BOUNDARY

Plates can also move sideways against each other. They slide in opposite directions or at different speeds, causing cracks, called faults, in the plates. These are conservative plate boundaries, because crust is neither gained nor lost.

MAPPING THE PLATES

The Earth's crust is made up of about nine large plates and twelve smaller ones. Do some research and see if you can mark the nine large plates on a map of the world.

The movements of the Earth's plates create cracks in the crust through which volcanoes can erupt. They also cause earthquakes as the rocks move and jolt past each other, making the ground shake.

On your map of the Earth's plates, mark the places where volcanic eruptions and earthquakes usually happen. You could devise a symbol to represent the volcanoes and the earthquakes. What do you notice about the distribution of volcanoes and earthquakes? Volcanoes around the Pacific Plate form a ring and so are known as the "ring of fire". Label this on your map, too.

HELPING HAND
You can find blank maps of the world on
www.EnchantedLearning.com/geography/continents/outlinemap

Volcanoes

Volcanoes are formed when magma from the Earth's mantle pours out through cracks in the Earth's crust. Once the magma is on the surface, it is called lava. Scientists estimate that there are over 1,500 active volcanoes around the globe, which may erupt at any time. A volcano that has not erupted for a long time is called a dormant volcano. An extinct volcano is one that should not erupt again.

WHEN A VOLCANO ERUPTS

Volcanoes are like valves, releasing the pressure of the gases that build up beneath the Earth's crust. The power of a volcanic eruption, and the shape of a volcano, depend mainly on how runny the magma is and the amount of gas trapped in it.

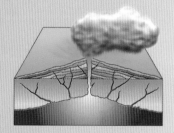

Shield volcano
If the magma is thin and runny, it forms wide, flat, shield volcanoes, such as the chain of volcanoes that make up the Hawaiian Islands.

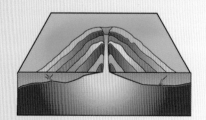

Dome volcano
Thick, sticky magma, moves slowly to the surface and cools quickly. This forms a tall, steep-sided cone that widens with every eruption.

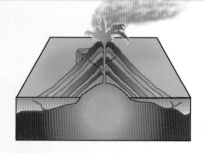

Composite volcano
Magma containing lots of gas bubbles explodes onto the surface. The main cone forms of ash and lava layers, with smaller secondary cones on the side.

VOLCANIC PLUGS

When the sides of the volcano have been worn away, the hardened lava in the central vent of a volcano may be left behind as a tall tower of rock. This is called a volcanic plug. There are several examples of volcanic plugs around the world. Try to find pictures of some of them. Start by looking for Devil's Tower, Wyoming, USA; Agathla Peak, Arizona, USA or the Chapel of St Michael d'Aguiche, which is situated on top of a volcanic plug in the French town of Le Puy, Auvergne.

VOLCANOES DATABASE

Build up a database of information about the world's volcanic eruptions, using sources such as information books, the Internet, newspaper articles and television documentaries. Collect information such as: the location of the volcano, the date of the eruption, the type of eruption, the damage caused to buildings, the effects (such as mud flows, ash falls and local climate change) and the number of people killed.

Think carefully about the best way to organise the information. You might choose to record the top ten biggest volcanic eruptions in history, or you might want to look at volcanoes that have erupted recently. Many islands are the tips of undersea volcanoes and most volcanoes erupt under the sea. You could include a column for undersea volcanoes in your database.

PREDICTING ERUPTIONS

About one in ten people live within the "danger zone" of an active volcano. To reduce the number of deaths caused by volcanic eruptions, it is important for scientists to monitor active volcanoes so they can evacuate people quickly before an eruption occurs. See if you can draw a chart of the different ways scientists monitor volcanoes, such as measuring the tilt of the Earth's surface, recording vibrations, measuring gases and taking the temperature of lava. Today, robots and other remote sensing devices make this monitoring safer than it used to be.

Inside the ancient volcanic cone of Mount Vesuvius, Italy.

KEY SKILLS
Collecting, recording and presenting data

Analysing information

Doing research

Mountains

Mountains are large landforms, with steep sloping sides, which are much higher than the land around them. Some geographers say that a mountain has to be over 1,000 metres high. Mountains make up one fifth of the Earth's land area and are also found under the sea. Some mountains stand on their own, but most are grouped together to form long mountain ranges, or chains, which can stretch for hundreds or even thousands of kilometres.

KEY SKILLS

Analysing information; asking geographical questions

Drawing maps

Collecting, recording and presenting evidence

Looking at mountains around the world

FOLD MOUNTAINS

Most of the world's mountains are formed as two crustal plates collide. They are called fold mountains because this movement pushes the crust upwards into gigantic folds.

BLOCK MOUNTAINS

Sometimes huge slabs of rock are pushed upwards to form block mountains. Examples of these include the Sierra Nevada mountain range in North America.

DOME MOUNTAINS

Magma rising from inside the Earth can force up the crust, without breaking through, to form dome mountains. The Black Hills, South Dakota, USA, are dome mountains.

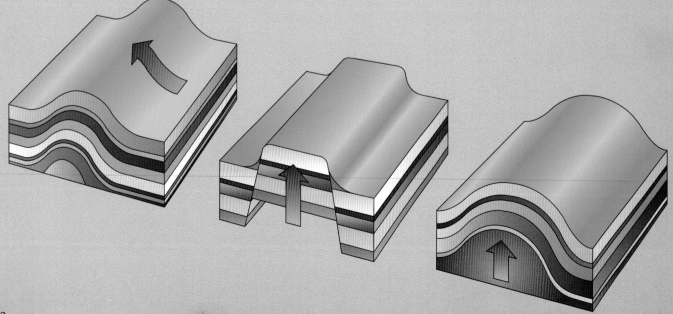

COMPARING MOUNTAINS

Mountains in different parts of the world have different characteristics. Choose two different mountain ranges, one in a less economically developed country (LEDC) and one in a more economically developed country (MEDC).

HELPING HAND
You could compare the Himalayas and the Alps or the Andes and the Rocky Mountains.

Draw a map to show the location of your two chosen mountain ranges. Then collect information from as many sources as possible. It is a good idea to decide on a list of features to compare. You may want to think about the following:

- how the mountains formed
- the size of the mountains
- the weather
- the landforms
- the wildlife and the people who live there.

PEOPLE WHO LIVE IN MOUNTAIN RANGES

Despite the harsh environment, about ten per cent of the world's population live in mountainous regions. How do people design their homes to cope with the severe mountain weather? Mountain people are often farmers, growing crops such as coffee or raising animals such as yaks or llamas. Some mountain people work in the tourist industry, helping skiers or mountaineers. How does mountain transport differ in the two mountain ranges you have studied?

The Himalaya Mountains are fold mountains, pushed up by India moving slowly northwards into the rest of Asia.

Earthquakes

Earthquakes occur when energy is suddenly released by plates as they move past each other. They cause the ground to shake violently. The point under the ground where an earthquake starts is called the focus. Vibrations, called seismic waves, spread out from the focus like ripples from a stone thrown into a pond.

SEISMIC WAVES

The power of the seismic waves depends on the depth of the focus, the strength of the rocks and how much they move. Body waves travel inside the Earth, while surface waves spread out from the epicentre, the point on the surface directly above the focus of the earthquake.

Most damage occurs at the epicentre of the earthquake. Huge cracks may appear in the land, swallowing up cars and buildings.

Large earthquakes can cause homelessness, unemployment and economic damage, across several countries. LEDCs take longer to recover because of their limited resources.

MEASURING QUAKES

The Richter scale measures the amount of energy released by an earthquake. Most serious earthquakes measure between five and nine on the Richter scale. The Kashmir/Pakistan earthquake of 2005 measured 7.6 on this scale. Each number on the scale is ten times more powerful than the one before and can be linked to the destruction it causes.

QUAKE REPORT

Find out as much as you can about a recent earthquake such as the one that hit parts of Kashmir and Pakistan in 2005; the Gujurat quake in India in 2001; the Izmit and Istanbul quake in Turkey in 1999; the Kobe quake in Japan in 1995.

Use your ICT skills to present your findings in the style of a newspaper report. How did the construction of the buildings affect the amount of damage caused by the quake?

Investigate what happened at the time of the quake and then look at the time taken to restore the power, water supply, infrastructure (such as roads, bridges and railways) and communications (such as telephone lines). Is the country where the quake happened an LEDC or an MEDC? How much help did the area receive from within its own country or other parts of the world? Has the country made plans to survive any future earthquakes?

The result of an earthquake in Turkey shows clearly how most buildings can quickly turn to rubble.

Rocks

The shape of landforms depends partly on the type of rocks from which they are formed. There are three main types of rock: igneous, sedimentary and metamorphic. Each type is formed over time by different processes and its characteristics affect the landscape in different ways.

KEY SKILLS
Collecting rock samples; completing a chart

Interpreting information

The white chalk cliffs of Dover, England, were formed from sediments that built up when this area was covered by water long ago.

DIFFERENT ROCK TYPES

Igneous rocks are formed from magma that cools and hardens, either on the Earth's surface or below ground. There are many examples of igneous formations around the world. These include the Giant's Causeway in Northern Ireland and the Devils' Marbles in Australia.

Most sedimentary rocks are formed from small pieces of other rocks (called sediments). These are carried away by wind or water and pressed together to form layered rocks. Some sedimentary rocks, such as chalk and limestone, are made of the remains of living creatures. Examples of sedimentary landforms include the Grand Canyon in Colorado, USA, and the White Cliffs of Dover, UK.

Metamorphic rocks are igneous or sedimentary rocks that have been changed by heat or pressure (or both) during volcanic activity or earth movements. Marble and slate are metamorphic.

THE ROCK CYCLE

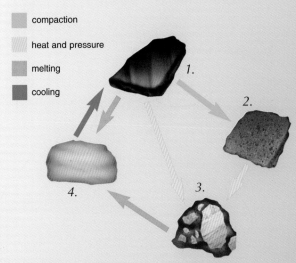

■ compaction

▨ heat and pressure

▨ melting

■ cooling

An igneous rock (1) can be changed first into a sedimentary rock (2), and then into a metamorphic rock (3), before melting to become magma (4) and cooling to become a new igneous rock. This recycling process is called the rock cycle. Many rocks do not complete every stage of the cycle.

ROCK COLLECTION

Try collecting small pieces of rock to build up your own rock collection. You could look for rocks, stones and pebbles in your garden, in the park or when you visit the country or the seaside. If you live in a town, you could take photographs of the different kinds of stone used in buildings. Look at the exhibits in some museums to find more ways that rocks have been used in the past. You might also be able to buy rock samples at the museum shop or at craft stores.

Store your rock collection in an old shoebox, using pieces of card to divide the box into sections. Put tissue or paper under your rock samples to protect them. Look in books or ask at museums to find out the names of the rocks and try to group them in three groups – igneous, sedimentary and metamorphic rocks.

When you have found out the names of your rocks, draw a table similar to the one below. Fill in information on each rock type, including what you discovered about them.

ROCK CHART

Type of rock	Name of rock	How it is used
Igneous	Granite, Basalt, Obsidian, Pumice	Tools and weapons, building stone, roads
Sedimentary		
Metamorphic		

Weathering

The natural breakdown of rocks at the Earth's surface is called weathering. The way that weathering changes the shape of the land depends on the climate and the type of rocks. Soft rocks, such as mudstone or chalk, wear away more easily than hard rocks, such as granite. Rain in heavy industrial areas often contains higher levels of acidity because of the pollution, and will wear away some stonework on buildings more quickly than cleaner rain.

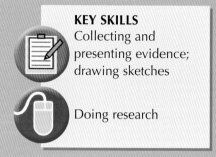

KEY SKILLS
Collecting and presenting evidence; drawing sketches

Doing research

TYPES OF WEATHERING

There are three main types of weathering: physical, chemical and biological.

Physical or mechanical weathering happens mainly when rocks heat up and expand by day, then cool down and contract at night. This makes the rocks crack and crumble so pieces break off or peel off. In cool, moist climates, ice sometimes forms in rock cracks at night, making the cracks wider.

Chemical weathering happens when rocks are eaten away by chemicals, such as the acids in rainwater. Limestone rocks are often weathered like this, especially along cracks or joints (see pages 24–25). Moist tropical climates encourage fast chemical weathering.

Biological weathering is the breakdown of rocks by plants and animals. Plant roots may be strong enough to enlarge cracks in rocks, while burrowing animals break up crumbling rocks.

SIGNS OF WEATHERING

See if you can find examples of weathering in your local area. Most towns have old buildings which often display obvious signs of chemical weathering. Look at the stonework around church windows or on the roof features, such as gargoyles. How have they been affected by chemical weathering? What has happened to the carved details? The same process is responsible for the breakdown of rocks in the natural environment.

Draw sketches and take photographs to record the examples you find. You could also use the Internet to find historical pictures of your area to show how parts of buildings have been weathered over time.

COMBINED ATTACK

Landforms are gradually broken down by a combination of different types of weathering. Look again at the photographs you took for your study of an old building. Can you see small, green or yellow plant growths on the stonework? These are called lichens and many of them release a mild acid which breaks down the surface so they can cling on. Look for lichens growing on rocks in gardens and parks.

The sandstone rocks of Bryce Canyon, USA, have been weathered and eroded by rain, wind, and snow to form pinnacles called hoodoos.

Erosion

Erosion is the wearing away of the land and the removal of weathered or loose material by wind, water and ice. The wind sweeps up debris and blasts it against the land (pages 22–23). Water in rivers carries stones that wear away the river bed and deposit material downstream (pages 26–31). The sea smashes huge waves against cliffs (pages 36–39) and ice grinds down rocks (pages 34–35).

KEY SKILLS

Interpreting information

Observing changes over time

The grass on this track has been slowly worn away by people walking on it. How could it be protected from further erosion?

A SLOW PROCESS

Erosion is a slow process that can only be recorded over a period of time – so you need to be patient. Most changes take years to become obvious.

SPEEDING UP EROSION

The effects of erosion can be speeded up, especially through human activity. Look at a well-used footpath in your local park or in the countryside. How has it been affected by people? Look for damage to vegetation and the structure of the top layer of soil. What do you think might happen if the erosion became worse? If there is stormy weather, such as heavy rain, strong winds or floods, you may notice big changes to the landscape in just a few days. Storms can wash away large amounts of soil and in some places cause landslides, when big pieces of land slip downhill. They can even make whole sections of cliff collapse.

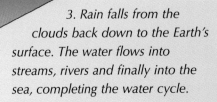

HELPING HAND
Think about the role that plants play in holding the soil together and reducing the effects of erosion.

THE WATER CYCLE

The shape of landforms changes all the time as water rains down from the sky, and rivers or oceans carry away pieces of rock. The movement of water between the sky and the surface of the Earth forms a continual cycle called the water cycle or the hydrological cycle ("hydro" means water). The amount of water on the Earth stays the same – it just moves from place to place.

1. The Sun heats water on the Earth's surface, turning some of it into water vapour, which disappears into the air. This process is called evaporation.

2. If the moist air rises and cools, the water vapour turns back into droplets of liquid water. This is called condensation. The condensed water droplets collect together to make clouds.

3. Rain falls from the clouds back down to the Earth's surface. The water flows into streams, rivers and finally into the sea, completing the water cycle.

Deserts

Deserts cover about one third of the Earth's land surface. There is usually less than 25 centimetres of rainfall a year in a desert and very few plants survive. High winds, extreme temperature changes and sudden floods of fast-flowing water erode the landscape, creating distinctive landforms. The landforms are also more visible without plants growing over them.

KEY SKILLS

Looking at deserts around the world

Doing research

Designing a poster

This desert landscape in Monument Valley, USA, has flat-topped islands of hard rock called mesas and columns of hard rock called buttes. ("Mesa" means table in Spanish.) They were probably shaped mainly by water erosion many years ago when the climate in the area was wetter. The softer rocks around the mesas and buttes have been eroded.

SHAPING THE LANDSCAPE

Desert sands are picked up by the wind and blown along just above the surface in a series of low hops. This process is called saltation. As the sharp grains of sand bounce along, they hit the rocks, wearing them away to form shapes such as arches and pillars. A rock shaped like a mushroom may form if layers of softer rock are worn away near the ground to form a narrow "stalk", but a wide, flat cap of harder rock remains balanced on top.

DESERT SURVIVAL

Deserts are very hostile environments for wildlife. Plants and animals have to survive boiling hot days and bitterly cold nights. Rain may not fall for months, or even years. Some desert animals do not drink at all. They get all the water they need from their food. Others, such as camels, store fat in their bodies to keep them going when food and water are hard to find. Where do plants such as cacti store water? Why do cacti have spines instead of leaves?

You are going to make a poster to show how plants and animals manage to adapt to desert conditions.

You could research desert wildlife in general and then create a poster with examples from one desert, or deserts in different parts of the world. You might want to concentrate on either plants or animals. You could even choose just one plant (such as a saguaro cactus) or one animal (such as a camel).

SAND DUNES

The wind blows desert sands into heaps called sand dunes. The shape of the dunes depends on the wind speed and direction, as well as the amount of sand and plant cover. The arrows on these illustrations show the direction of the wind.

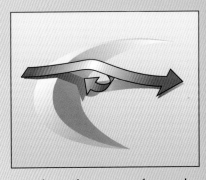

Barchan dunes are formed around obstacles.

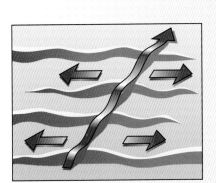

Seif dunes are formed by crosswinds, and are long and gently curving.

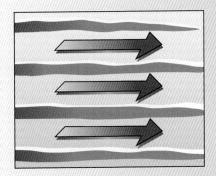

Linear dunes form when the wind blows from one direction.

Star dunes are formed where the wind blows from different directions.

Limestone landscapes

Areas with limestone rocks produce a landscape called karst scenery. There is very little water flowing on the surface of this landscape. Rainwater slowly dissolves the joints in the soft limestone rock to form separate slabs which form a "limestone pavement". The water flows underground through large gaps between the rocks, called swallow holes, or sinkholes, forming underground rivers.

KEY SKILLS

Researching limestone quarries

Interpreting information

Writing a report

This limestone pavement is in Ireland. A limestone pavement is made up of blocks of limestone called clints, with cracks between the blocks, called grykes.

Spectacular stalactites and stalagmites in Carlsbad Cavern, New Mexico, USA.

A LIMESTONE CAVE SYSTEM

Rainwater contains acid that dissolves calcium carbonate, the main ingredient found in limestone. Once the water is below the surface and flowing along lines of weakness in the rock, it hollows out passages and caves. Rainwater can dissolve only a few millimetres of limestone in a year so a large cave system takes thousands of years to form.

As water seeping through the cave evaporates, it leaves behind drips of watery rock that build up to form stalactites, which hang from the roof of the cave, and pillars, called stalagmites, which "grow" upwards from the floor of the cave.

QUARRYING CONFLICT

Limestone is quarried to provide building stone. It is also used as a fertiliser to help crops grow, to make cement and to make steel.

Limestone quarrying can cause conflicts between the quarry company, the local people, the tourist industry and environmental groups. Find out some of the arguments for and against quarrying and write a report explaining your findings.

You may find the following arguments for quarrying useful:

- It provides raw materials needed for building and industry

- When the quarry is closed, the hole can be filled with water to make a lake for wildlife and sports.

Some of the arguments against quarrying are:

- It produces a lot of noise and dust, which reduces the quality of the environment and stops tourists visiting the area
- It increases the amount of dangerous traffic, especially large lorries transporting the stone.

HELPING HAND
Log on to
www.goodquarry.com to find
out more about quarries.

25

Rivers at work

Rivers are natural channels in the landscape that carry water downhill to the sea. As rivers flow along they erode the land, carrying material away and depositing it somewhere else. The way that rivers shape the land depends on how fast they flow and the sort of rocks they flow over.

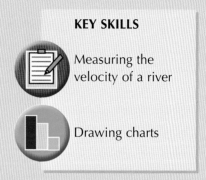
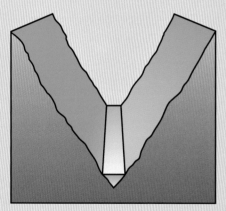

A narrow V-shaped valley in the upper course of a river.

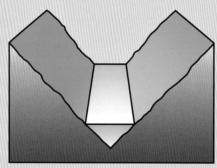

A wider V-shaped valley in the middle course of a river.

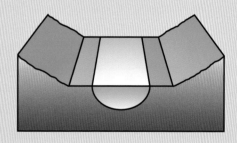

A wide, flat valley in the lower course of a river.

VALLEY SHAPES

At the source of a river, along its upper course, the water cuts downwards into the land, forming a narrow, V-shaped valley with steep sides.

In the middle of a river, the water cuts both downwards and sideways, forming a wider, V-shaped valley.

Towards the end of a river, near its mouth, the water cuts sideways and also deposits material, forming a wide, flat valley.

A RIVER'S LOAD

The material a river carries is called its load. A river moves, or transports, its load in three main ways:

- Some particles are dissolved in the water, so they are invisible.
- Fine particles, silt or clay hang or float in the water and are carried along by the water itself.
- Larger particles, such as stones, pebbles and rocks, roll, slide or bounce along the bottom of the river.

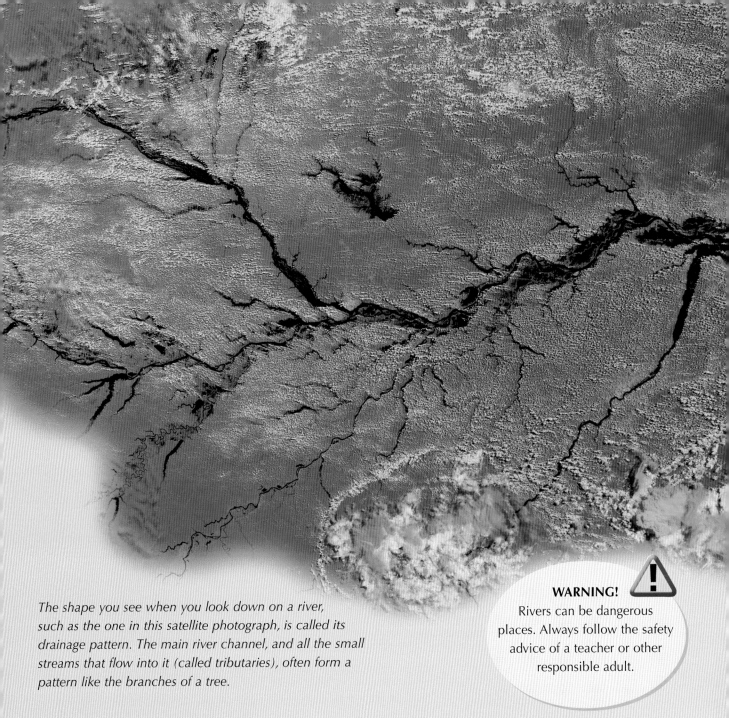

The shape you see when you look down on a river, such as the one in this satellite photograph, is called its drainage pattern. The main river channel, and all the small streams that flow into it (called tributaries), often form a pattern like the branches of a tree.

WARNING!
Rivers can be dangerous places. Always follow the safety advice of a teacher or other responsible adult.

HOW FAST DO RIVERS FLOW?

To measure the speed of your local stream or river, see how fast an object floats over a certain distance. Use twigs or stones to mark a distance of 100 metres along the bank. Drop a stick into the water by one marker and time how long it takes to float down to the other marker. Watch how the sticks flow around bends in the stream or river. Do the sticks flow faster in some places than others?

To calculate the speed of water flow, called the velocity, you need to divide the distance by the time. Measure the speed at different places and draw a chart to compare your results. A fairly fast river flows at about 5 kilometres per hour. During a flood, rivers flow much faster, sometimes at more than 25 kilometres per hour. The speed of a stream or river depends partly on the downhill slope of the riverbed, called the gradient. It also depends on the shape of the channel and whether it is rough or smooth.

The upper river

The beginning of a river is called its source. Many rivers have their source in the mountains. Others start flowing from a natural hollow in the ground, or perhaps a lake, a marsh or a melting glacier.

INTERLOCKING SPURS

At first, the river runs through a deep, narrow valley, winding around areas of hard rock and eroding the softer rock. The erosion causes ridges of land to stick out into the river valley. These ridges are called interlocking spurs.

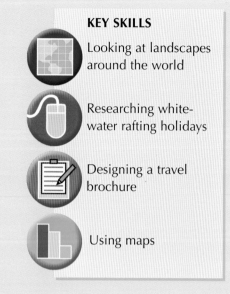

KEY SKILLS

Looking at landscapes around the world

Researching white-water rafting holidays

Designing a travel brochure

Using maps

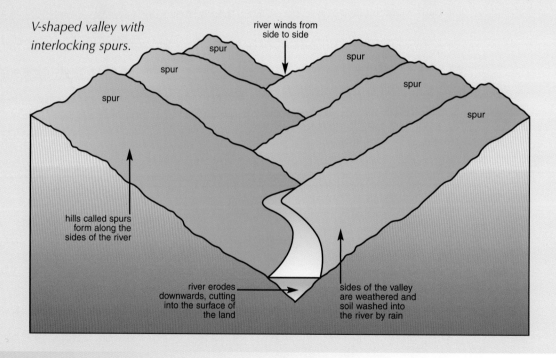

V-shaped valley with interlocking spurs.

river winds from side to side

spur

spur

spur

spur

spur

spur

hills called spurs form along the sides of the river

river erodes downwards, cutting into the surface of the land

sides of the valley are weathered and soil washed into the river by rain

WATERFALLS AND RAPIDS

Waterfalls and rapids are characteristic features of the upper river. A waterfall occurs where the river flows over a band of hard rock with softer rock on the other side. The softer rock wears away, leaving a large step of rock, over which the water falls in a foaming cascade. The force of the falling water may carve out a deep plunge pool at the base of the waterfall. Rapids form where bands of hard and soft rock break up the flow of the water in a series of small steps.

DESIGN A TRAVEL BROCHURE

The water flowing over rapids in the upper river foams and splashes to make patches of white, frothy water. It is exciting to travel over this "white water" in an inflatable boat or a canoe. This is called white-water rafting. You are going to design a travel brochure advertising a white-water rafting holiday.

Research these activity holidays on the Internet or at a travel agent's and find out in which parts of the world they take place. Describe and illustrate the river landscape and remember to include a map, details of travel arrangements and accommodation. How fast does the boat go? What sorts of safety measures have to be taken? How does a tourist activity like this affect the river landscape?

The Iguaçu Falls, on the border between Argentina and Brazil, are the widest waterfalls in the world, stretching for about 3.2 kilometres. The waterfall system consists of almost 300 falls, which are up to 70 metres tall. More than one million people visit the falls every year.

HELPING HAND
Try to make your leaflet as interesting and exciting as possible to entice people to book your holiday.

The middle and lower river

As a river flows further away from its source, it carries more water and sediment. It also begins to deposit some of its load, creating different features on the landscape.

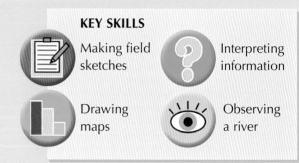
MEANDERS

The course of the river begins to twist from side to side, forming loops or bends called meanders. Sometimes, the river cuts through the narrow neck of land in the middle of a big meander loop. A U-shaped lake is left behind. It is called an ox-bow lake after the name for the U-shaped collar of an ox's yoke.

Eventually, the river flows across an almost flat plain, which is often flooded when the river spills over its banks. When the river reaches the sea, it slows down and drops the rest of its load. A new piece of land called a delta may form.

The River Amazon meanders across its flat valley floor in South America. Thick rainforest grows right up to the edge of the river.

DELTAS

A delta develops when a river drops its sediment faster than the sea can carry it away. The shape of a delta depends on how much water and sediment is in the river, and how fast the river is flowing. It also depends on the speed and strength of the waves, currents and tides in the sea.

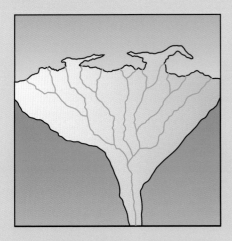

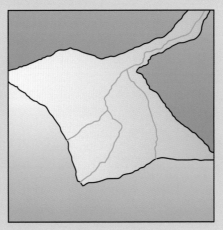

Arcuate (triangle shape) deltas form when the sea has weak waves, currents and tides. The Nile river delta in Egypt is an arcuate delta.

Cuspate (tooth shape) deltas form when the sea has strong waves and currents. The Tiber river delta in Italy is a cuspate delta.

Bird's foot deltas form in calm seawater when the river is carrying a lot of sediment. The Mississippi river delta in the USA is a bird's foot delta.

RECORDING RIVERS

If you have a shallow river in your local area, you may be able to make a field sketch of a meander or part of its course. If you can stand on higher ground above the river, it will make it easier to see the shape of its channel. Look out for these features:

- A river cliff – the river flows fastest on the outside bend of a meander and may cut into the banks to form a river cliff.
- A river beach – on the inside bend, the river flows more slowly and deposits some of the material it is carrying. The material may build up to form a river beach.

Identify these features on your field sketch using labels. You could also draw a cross-section of the river bed to show clearly how it is shaped by the flowing water.

If you do not live near a river, you could look at the rivers already recorded on maps. See if you can identify some of the features typical of a middle or lower stage river, such as: wide rivers, flat river valleys, meanders, ox-bow lakes, floodplains and deltas. You could also draw your own map of an imaginary river, showing the different features you would find as you went on a journey from the source of the river to the sea.

River flooding

River flooding happens when the amount of water in the river suddenly rises and spills over the banks. Floods are often caused by sudden heavy rainfall or snow melting rapidly in spring. They are also caused by water draining very quickly from towns and cities. Global warming is changing the weather and may cause more floods in the future.

The Three Gorges Dam, due to be completed by 2009, will be two kilometres wide and about 183 metres high. It stretches across the world's third longest river, the Yangtze, in China. It will help to generate hydro-electricity and reduce flooding.

FLOOD CONTROL

To reduce the damage caused by river flooding, engineers build dams and high riverbanks, called levées, to control the flow of water. This is known as hard engineering. They also make river channels deeper or straighter so they will carry more water away quickly. These hard engineering solutions change the natural river flow, affecting the environment and often causing flooding problems further down the river.

Soft engineering solutions tackle flooding using more natural methods. These include planting trees to soak up water, using walls of sandbags to hold back the water and channelling rainwater into the soil, lakes or ponds. Predicting floods, and preventing new building in areas at risk from flooding, is also important.

Dramatic air rescue in Mozambique. Helicopters are sometimes the only way of rescuing people trapped by rising flood waters.

HELPING HAND
This website will help you find out more about serious floods.
http://news.bbc.co.uk/1/hi/world/africa/655227.stm

AFTER THE FLOOD

A flood disaster can sometimes kill hundreds or even thousands of people. The water, and the mud and debris the flood water carries, damages homes, ruins crops, destroys factories and makes it difficult to use roads, railways or airports – if they survive the flood. If sewage contaminates the water, then diseases such as cholera can spread quickly causing many more deaths.

Floods occur in both LEDCs and MEDCs, but the effects are usually worse in LEDCs because the flood warning systems, flood defences and flood recovery programmes are not as efficient or as well funded. You are going to research a flood, such as the Mozambique floods of 2000. Find out about what happened during the flood and the problems faced by the people of Mozambique afterwards.

Using this information, design a fund-raising leaflet or poster to alert people to the problems faced by flood victims in an LEDC. What sort of pictures would make people give as much money as possible? Give some examples of how the money would be used, such as restoring freshwater supplies or providing medicines. What would be the best ways of dealing with more floods in the future?

Ice at work

Ice covers about ten per cent of the Earth's surface, mainly at the Poles and on high mountains. Some land is covered by huge layers of ice, called ice sheets, while "rivers" of ice, called glaciers, sometimes form in mountain valleys. As the ice moves slowly downhill, it drags rocks and pebbles with it, and carves the land into new shapes. When the ice melts, it leaves behind ridges, hummocks and gravel-covered plains, called outwash plains.

KEY SKILLS

 Using maps and atlases

 Explaining geographical features and processes

 Drawing sketches; making models

LAND SHAPED BY ICE

The enormous size and weight of the glacier ice:

- Carves the shape of the V-shaped valley into a straighter, U-shape
- Digs out great hollows, called corries
- Cuts off spurs of land
- Drops and shapes egg-shaped mounds, called drumlins.

When the glacier ice melts and recedes it:

- Leaves small tributary river valleys "hanging" high above the valley floor
- Leaves behind curved ridges of rock and rubble called moraines, which are where the sides or the end of the glacier used to be
- Leaves behind blocks of melted ice that may form hollows full of water, called kettle holes.

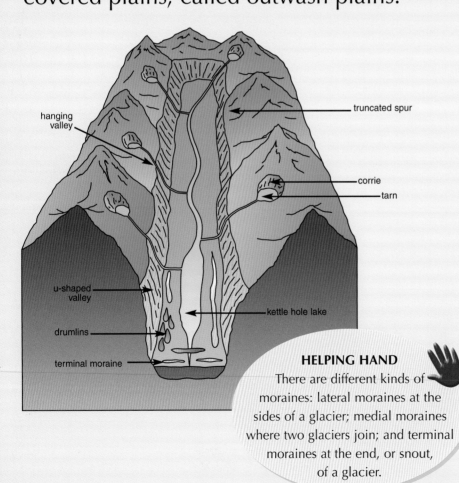

hanging valley

truncated spur

corrie

tarn

u-shaped valley

kettle hole lake

drumlins

terminal moraine

HELPING HAND
There are different kinds of moraines: lateral moraines at the sides of a glacier; medial moraines where two glaciers join; and terminal moraines at the end, or snout, of a glacier.

MAP SPOTTING

Use an atlas or the Internet to find a map of an area featuring glaciers, such as the Columbia Icefield in Canada. Try to identify landforms that were shaped by the power of the ice at work. Here are some clues to look for:

- Wide, flat valleys with a small river in the middle
- Straight valleys with steep sides
- Side valleys that seem to be cut off where they join the edge of a main valley
- Waterfalls coming from "hanging valleys" down the sides of a main valley
- Small lakes, or tarns, near the top of mountains. These may be where water has collected in a corrie
- A steep peak, called a pyramidal peak, with several corries around it, at the top of a mountain.

Then draw a sketch or make a model to show what the landscape would look like if you visited the area on your map.

This glacier is in Alaska, USA. Huge cliffs of ice form on the coast where a glacier or an ice sheet flows into the sea.

Shaping the coast

Where the land meets the sea, the pounding waves create unique coastal landforms. As the waves hurl stones and pebbles against the shore, they wear the rocks away. The waves also force air and water into cracks in the rocks, bursting them apart. Seawater causes a chemical reaction in some rocks that slowly dissolves them. Material produced by all these processes of erosion, together with sediment deposited on the coast by rivers, is transported up, down and along the coast by the waves.

HOW WAVES FORM

Most waves are caused by the wind whipping up the surface of the sea to make little peaks of water. Inside each peak the water moves round in circles. The size and speed of waves depends on the strength of the wind, the length of time that the wind blows and the distance the wave travels. Near the coast, the waves slow down in the shallow water, causing the top of the wave to topple over and break on the shore.

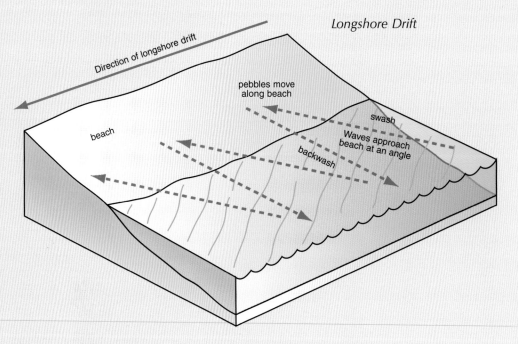

Longshore Drift

Direction of longshore drift

pebbles move along beach

swash

Waves approach beach at an angle

beach

backwash

WAVE TRANSPORT

If waves hit a beach at an angle, they gradually move the beach material sideways in a zig-zag path. This is called longshore drift, because the material slowly drifts along the shore.

WAVE WATCHING

On a visit to the coast, watch how the waves pick up sand, rocks and pebbles and move them around. As the stones and pebbles smash into each other, they break into smaller and smaller pieces. Jagged rocks turn into smooth, round pebbles, or eventually small grains of shingle and sand. You could collect pebbles from different levels on the beach and measure their sizes.

Look to see how the waves hit the shore. Do they come straight towards the shore, or are they at an angle?

In places where longshore drift happens, people sometimes build wooden barriers, called groynes, at right angles to the coastline. The groynes stop beach material being carried along the coast, so the beach protects the coast from further erosion.

Use the Internet to find pictures of groynes. Make a sketch of the groynes. Why does beach material build up on one side of the groyne? What happens further along the coast, where beach material is no longer being deposited because of the groynes?

HELPING HAND

Here are some useful coastal erosion words:

Corrasion – waves throwing broken rocks against the coast

Corrosion – seawater dissolving or rotting rocks chemically

Attrition – rock fragments grinding each other down.

Waves breaking on the shore have immense power and create a foamy mass of white surf. Here, water moves up and down the beach rather than round and round in circles.

Wearing away coasts

Over long periods of time, wave erosion wears the coast away, forming features such as cliffs, sea caves and rock arches. Soft rock wears away faster than hard rock to form bays, with harder rocks sticking out to form points of land called headlands. As the headlands are worn away and material is deposited in the bays, the coastline is gradually smoothed out.

The Twelve Apostles are a series of spectacular limestone stacks off the coast of southeast Australia. These tall pillars of rock mark the position of the original coastline, before it was eroded.

WAVE-CUT PLATFORM

Some beaches have a wide, flat area of rock at the base of the cliffs. This is called a wave-cut platform. It forms when waves cut into the bottom of the cliff, making the cliff collapse. Once the waves have removed the cliff material, the flat platform is left behind.

HELPING HAND
You can find out more about erosion on pages 20, 21, 36 and 37 and more about coastal landforms on pages 40 and 41.

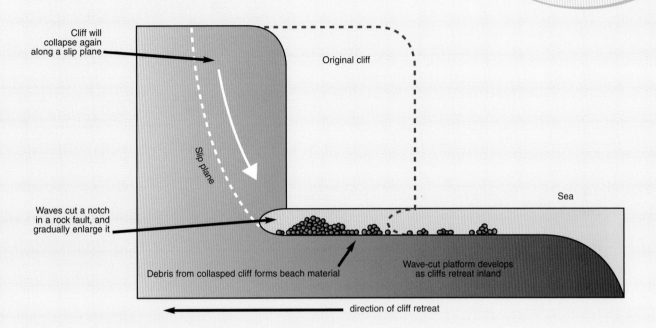

Cliff will collapse again along a slip plane

Original cliff

Slip plane

Sea

Waves cut a notch in a rock fault, and gradually enlarge it

Debris from collasped cliff forms beach material

Wave-cut platform develops as cliffs retreat inland

direction of cliff retreat

FROM CAVES AND ARCHES TO STACKS AND STUMPS

As waves crash against a narrow crack in a headland, they may erode the rock to form a sea cave. If waves cut right through a headland, a narrow bridge called a rock arch forms. If the top of the arch collapses, a pillar of rock, called a stack, remains. A stack itself may collapse into a stump.

COASTAL WALK

Find a map of a coastal area with some footpaths and interesting landforms, such as south Victoria in Australia.

Design a leaflet showing the coastal walks people could take from a central point, such as a car park or a tourist information centre.

On your leaflet, include a sketch map of the area, with dotted lines for the different walks. You could draw short walks and long walks in different colours and explain in the key to the map how long the walks will take.

At the sides of the map, draw some diagrams showing how the sea formed the coastal features. Point out any other

interesting features, such as offshore islands, or nearby hills or towns you would be able to see in the distance. Mark on rest stops with good views and the best places to take photographs.

In a separate box, draw attention to safety factors, such as:

- Do not go too near the edge of a cliff; it might crumble away
- Cliffs are exposed to the weather. Take warm or waterproof clothing with you, if necessary.

Building up coasts

Some coastal landforms are created when the sea transports loose material along the shore to form beaches or long ridges of sand and shingle. Larger rocks and pebbles are rolled or bounced along by the waves. Smaller particles of sand and mud float in the water, while salts and other chemicals are dissolved in the seawater.

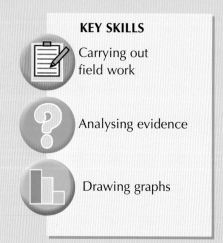
SPITS AND TOMBOLOS

If there is a break in a coastline, such as where the coast changes direction, or at the mouth of a river, longshore drift may push beach material out into the sea. This forms a long, thin ridge called a spit. The waves may push the end of a spit into a curved shape, called a recurved spit.

Sometimes, a spit may link up with an island. This sand or shingle bridge linking the island to the mainland is called a tombolo.

MEASURING BEACHES

On a visit to the seaside, you could measure the angle of slope of the beach and draw a beach profile. The quickest and easiest way to measure the angle of a slope is to use a clinometer. If you do not have a clinometer, which can be bought from a surveying equipment shop, you can easily make your own.

MAKING A CLINOMETER

Draw a semi-circle on a piece of thick card and cut it out. Use a protractor to mark off degrees on the card, with 0° in the middle and 90° at each end. Tie a small weight to one end of a short piece of string and tie the other end to a short length of thin dowel. Tape the dowel firmly to the straight edge of your card so the string swings freely from a point in the middle of the card.

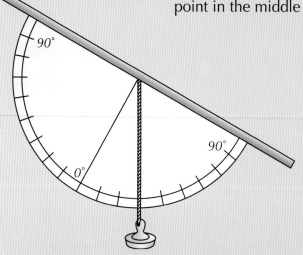

This is what your finished clinometer should look like. Ask a friend to read off the number once the string has stopped swinging. The number is the angle of the slope.

ON THE BEACH

Ask a friend to stand at the top of the beach. Take the clinometer a little way down the slope of the beach and look straight along the dowel rod at your friend's nose. Ask another friend to record the angle where the string crosses the scale. Measure the distance between where the two of you are standing. Then do the same thing at other points further down the slope. Using your results, draw a graph to show the beach profile, with distance along the base of the graph (horizontal axis) and angle of slope up the side (vertical axis).

This series of sandy, delta islands is in north Queensland, Australia. You can see a light-coloured spit (top, left) being formed by longshore drift.

Managing coasts

About three-quarters of the world's people live on or near coasts. Natural processes of coastal erosion often threaten their homes and livelihoods. Coastlines can also be damaged by storms, hurricanes or natural disasters such as tsunamis. Global warming is causing sea levels to rise, putting more coastlines at risk from flooding in the future.

KEY SKILLS

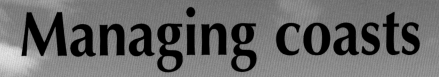

Interpreting information

Writing a formal letter

PROTECTING THE COAST

Coastal communities try to protect themselves from the wind and the waves in a variety of ways. Hard engineering solutions to flooding and erosion use barriers to hold back the sea, or absorb the energy of the waves. The barriers include fences called groynes (see pages 36 and 37), sea walls, revetments (slatted barriers, left) and gabions (steel mesh cages full of boulders). These barriers cost a lot of money and are only a temporary solution to the problem. They often increase erosion further along the coast.

Soft engineering solutions involve building up and conserving beaches, dunes, marshes and mangrove swamps near the coast to increase the natural protection along the shoreline. The coast is allowed to erode naturally, moving houses as necessary and building new houses further inland.

(LEFT) Revetments (such as these at Prestatyn, north Wales) help to reduce the force of the waves and reduce coastal erosion. They protect the coast more than a sea wall but they upset the natural beauty of a coastal area.

LIVING NEAR A CLIFF

Imagine you live in a house near the edge of a cliff. The sea is eroding the cliff and the edge of the cliff is now only 50 metres away from your home. Houses near where you live have already fallen down the cliff. You are about to write a letter to the local council asking them to do more about protecting the coast. What points would you make in the letter?

Think about how much coastal defences would cost. Do you think a hard engineering solution or a soft engineering solution would best solve your problem?

This house has become a victim of coastal erosion and people can no longer live in it.

What arguments would you use to persuade the council to act quickly? Would the defences reassure tourists and help to attract them to the area? Are there any public buildings, such as schools, churches or libraries close by?

Perhaps you could include some photographs, maps and diagrams to show how bad the problem is. Would you be prepared to move house if the cliff could not be protected against the sea? You could ask if the council would be prepared to pay you compensation for having to move.

Glossary

Cholera
A severe, life-threatening bacterial infection of the small intestine, usually caused by contaminated water or food.

Clinometer
A device for measuring the angle and height of a slope.

Continental drift
The way the continents slowly drift about the globe because of powerful forces deep inside the Earth.

Contour line
A line on a map, which joins places that are the same height above sea level.

Corrie
A deep hollow scraped out by the ice at the start of a glacier. Corries are also known as cirques or cwms.

Delta
A mass of alluvium (muddy river sediment), which is often triangular in shape, found at the mouth of a river.

Deposit
When a river or the sea puts sediment down.

Drumlin
A smooth mound of glacial debris, usually shaped like an egg. Drumlins often occur in groups.

Epicentre
The point on the Earth's surface directly above the focus of an earthquake.

Erosion
The loosening of weathered material and the carrying away of this material by the wind, water (rivers or the sea) or ice (glaciers).

Floodplain
The wide, flat valley floor, characteristic of the lower course of a river, which is often flooded by river water.

Global warming
A gradual increase in the average temperature of the Earth's atmosphere.

Groynes
Fence-like structures on a beach, which trap sand or pebbles and reduce longshore drift.

Hard engineering
Building structures to control geographical processes, such as river flooding or coastal erosion.

Igneous rock
A rock formed when magma cools and hardens underground or lava cools and hardens on the Earth's surface.

Lava
Molten rock on the Earth's surface.

Less economically developed country (LEDC)
A country in which the majority of the population lives in poverty. These countries tend to be mainly rural, but often their cities are growing fast.

Longshore drift
The movement of sediment along the shore when waves strike the shore at an angle.

Magma
Rock in a hot, molten state deep below the Earth's surface.

Meanders
Large bends in a river, formed by erosion and deposition.

Metamorphic rock
A rock formed when igneous or sedimentary rocks are altered by heat or pressure, or both.

Moraines
Piles of boulders, rocks, pebbles and soil carried along by a glacier, or left behind when a glacier has melted.

More economically developed country (MEDC)
A country with much greater wealth per person and more developed industry than a less economically developed country.

Mouth
Where a river enters the sea.

River course
The channel of a river.

Sediment
Rock debris that is carried or deposited by water, ice or wind.

Sedimentary rock
A layered rock that forms from the debris of other rocks and the remains of plants or animals.

Silt
Tiny grains or particles of rock.

Soft engineering
Using natural environmental processes to cope with geographical problems, such as flooding or coastal erosion.

Spit
A finger-like ridge of sediment joined to coastal land at one end, but extending out into open water.

Stack
A tall pillar of rock left behind when the sea erodes a headland.

Tombolo
A sand bridge linking an island with the mainland.

Tsunami
A huge sea wave triggered by an undersea earthquake.

Weathering
The gradual breakdown of rocks on the Earth's surface by the weather, by plants and animals or by chemicals.

Weblinks

http://earth.google.com
Download free aerial photographs and the corresponding map of any location in the world.

http://library.thinkquest.org/17457/english.html
Well-illustrated site, with information about the Earth's crustal plates and a volcanoes database.

http://en.wikipedia.org/wiki/Mountain
Facts and figures about mountains, together with photographs of mountains around the world.

http://quake.usgs.gov
Maps, research, preparing for earthquakes, the latest quake information and weblinks to other sites.

http://ga.water.usgs.gov/edu/earthglacier.html
Water science for schools, including the water cycle, glaciers and icecaps, glaciers in the landscape and Ice Ages.

www.enchantedlearning.com/geography/rivers
Information on how rivers work, major rivers of the world (including maps), US rivers and the water cycle.

www.irn.org
Website for the International Rivers Network, which protects rivers and defends the rights of people who depend on them.

http://www.ga.gov.au/education/facts/landforms
Information on Australian landforms, including Uluru, mountains, rivers, islands, waterfalls and deserts.

Note to parents and teachers:

Every effort has been made by the Publishers to ensure that these websites are suitable for children, that they are of the highest educational value, and that they contain no inappropriate or offensive material. However, because of the nature of the Internet, it is impossible to guarantee that the contents of these sites will not be altered. We strongly advise that Internet access is supervised by a responsible adult.

Index